The Historic Accomplishment of Karl Marx

The Historic Accomplishment of Karl Marx

Karl Kautsky

Cosmonaut International Translation Series Vol. I

Translator's Introduction

Karl Kautsky lived and wrote in a world and time when the growing organizational strength of the proletariat seemed to point inevitably towards communist society. In 1908, at the time that Kautsky wrote *The Historic Accomplishment of Karl Marx*, German revolutionary Social-Democracy was at the height of its power, having in the year prior won almost a third of all votes in the German federal election; and by all accounts, so was Kautsky himself at 53 years of age. As the foremost theoretician of Social-Democracy, he would go on to write three of his most memorable and influential books within that and the following year. German Social-Democracy, as the country's largest party, seemed inevitably poised to take power, not only in the dreams of its hundreds of thousands of dedicated Marxist members but in the nightmares and diaries of the ruling classes. The growing and entrenched socialist opposition parties in the more or less advanced industrial nations, including Germany and the 25 other parties that made up the Second International, were a living testament to the prophecy and promise of Marxism.

The demonstrative vigor and organizational strength of the working class at that moment can understandably appear to many today as a distant memory, like a dream that one struggles to remember. In the midst of a historic pandemic and global health crisis, and after decades of decline for the power of organized labor, millions of workers feel isolated and powerless to change the hazardous and cruel conditions of work forced upon them, not to speak of radically transforming society itself. Due to the impotent nature of our thoroughly debt-burdened capitalist economy and the developing economic depression, it appears unlikely that there will be relief anytime soon for most of the millions of Americans who have been laid off. But while the forced closure of most non-essential businesses, undertaken (far too late) in order to slow the spread of the coronavirus, has left an unprecedented number of Americans unemployed, countless workers in essential economic sectors have realized their ability and the desperate need to fight for better conditions of work. The crisis is so blatantly a disaster exacerbated by the greedy callousness of big business that many workers are now protesting and organizing to preserve their health, and indeed their lives.

In a time like this, there is a pressing need to articulate the idea that there is and ought to be more to the working class's struggle than straightforward economic concessions won from employers. It is certainly true that the most direct and palpable struggle of the individual worker resisting exploitation in the hospital, factory, shipping and fulfillment center, or grocery store is the arena from which the most elementary class awareness springs. However, this most reliable and elementary class awareness attained by the millions through organizing in the economic struggle must be developed and brought to higher forms of awareness through agitation, education and other forms of organization. As Marxists we believe that the short-sighted system of capitalism is governed by laws which in effect doom it to repeat the catastrophes of economic and social crisis, with the ensuing senseless human suffering, year after year, decade after decade. Only a historic "catastrophe" in the form of a consciously political social revolution, the takeover of all levels of society by the proletariat, can win against the true catastrophes flung by capitalism against life itself.

With the fall of the USSR and actually-existing socialism, capitalism with its American militarism has engulfed the world in its cynical debt-fueled logic and threatens to fully incinerate it in more ways than one — economic collapse, climate change, disease, war, etc. Imperialism, the subjugation of the world's weaker economies and peoples by the wealthier ones, is unfortunately (contrary to deep-rooted bourgeois and chauvinist sentiment) as powerful a world force as ever. Predatory business plans and loans to the third world, demanding steep interest payments, incessantly threaten to extinguish human development and the lives of hundreds of millions of human beings. When workers of the first world suffer with economic collapse, workers of the third world die. As a consequence of this unfolding global system, with nothing but negligent contempt for the human being, we have seen a resurgence of working-class resistance and rebellion that could be called historic in its size and tenacity. From the Andes mountains of Latin America to the Western Ghats of India, militant resistance of hundreds of millions of workers in the global south to the violations of their political rights and economic interests has rekindled the flames of class struggle many had thought extinguished. Within the "core" countries of Western Europe and North America, there are now also hopeful signs of a comeback of a militant and courageous working class.

In the wake of the turmoil of the Great Recession and perpetually rising inequality, Karl Marx became a figure that appeared *not only* on the radical left as an admirable or at least valuable thinker. To the extent that Marxism has so far made a comeback in western societies, the truth of the matter is that it has made it only on the outskirts of the organized working class; it has made it on the fringes of bourgeois academia, among isolated intellectuals, and has found attraction once more in a section of the petty-bourgeoisie. Unfortunately, the majority of organized union members in the United States are often seen on the radical left as undesirable targets of socialist agitation, education, and organization. While America's union membership rate may still be at historic lows, levels almost not seen since before the Great Depression of the 1930s, income inequality has been perpetually on the rise while hazardous conditions of work are now being faced by many workers with few benefits. The economic and political future of this country is, by almost all accounts and commentaries, troublesome. If the left and a project for the liberation of humanity is to prevail over the bourgeois alternatives akin to one sort or another of exploitative authoritarianism or fascism, it will require a large and unprecedented effort certain of its scientific outlook.

Karl Kautsky's summation and lessons in this book, vital not only to a historical understanding of Marxism but to the actual project of changing the world, give us an example of this outlook. Born to a German mother and Czech father in Prague, Kautsky went on to study in Vienna, where he became a member of the Social-Democratic Party. Moving to Zurich in 1880 during the time of the German Empire's anti-socialist laws, Kautsky helped smuggle propaganda over the border and met Eduard Bernstein. Soon after becoming friends with Friedrich Engels and visiting him and Marx in England, Kautsky started the journal *Die Neue Zeit* in 1883. As the man whom Lenin called "the Pope of Marxism," Kautsky rose to prominence when the German Social-Democratic Party asked him to draft the party's groundbreaking Erfurt Program in 1891. It was this revolutionary and Marxist minimum–maximum program which demanded and upheld the loyalties of the broad spectrum of Social-Democratic Party members for decades.

It is something of an understatement to say that it is not enough to simply have faith that history is on our side and that the contradictions of capitalism will do our work for us. This is hopefully becoming more and more clear, not only because of the obvious fact that the working class needs to be prepared in a myriad ways to effectively govern, but because crises and upticks in labor militancy do not in fact equate by themselves to political unity of the class. Nor do unreachable demands by socialist radicals in the labor movement, through transitional demands or calls for an immediate general strike, help to develop a common goal for the class. Such demands and proposals to the working class are unfortunately attractive to many because of their expedient substitution for the patient work of Marxist agitation, education, and political organization. Beside their evidentiary historical unviability as means for the working class to actually win power (without the necessary prerequisites at the very least), calls for transitional demands and other such measures function as shortcuts and are more often than not excuses for a lack of willingness to enter into often unpopular contradiction with popular desires and impulses.

It is as well hard to fathom in what world the entrenched oppositional politics to be found throughout most of Karl Kautsky's life can be used to justify a politics today which passes as "Kautskyist" while openly celebrating class collaboration and advancing the concept of winning "hegemony" within the existing bourgeois state. If anything, the biggest strength of Karl Kautsky's thought lies in his oppositional strategy of patience, the commitment to the building of a mass party and the development of a communist program. For comrades today to, on the one hand, sing Kautsky's praises and claim to "uphold" his legacy while on the other encouraging socialists to tail bourgeois campaigns and aspire to positions in bourgeois government is problematic to say the least. Surely what has been lacking so far has not been a rudimentary socialist sympathy among the people, of which there is plenty, even though organized labor has yet to benefit from this impressively growing sympathy.

America's largest union, the AFL-CIO, currently has a reported annual revenue of $113 million. As released reports have shown, the presidency of Richard Trumpka has seen the union spend less than ten percent of its revenue on actual organizing last year.[i] At the same time, millions upon millions of members' dollars were spent on venal political contributions and lavish salaries for bureaucrats. If organized labor wants to reawaken from its slumber, it needs to reorient itself towards class struggle, and this means class unity. As Kautsky makes clear, it is socialist theory which is vital in building a mass conception and reality of class unity. Marxists today who reject industrial organizing and coordinated revolutionary activity within unions demonstrate narrow theoretical obsessions at best, or cynical treason to the fate and promise of our working people at worst. While there are still real differences among Marxists on issues that can and must not be glossed over, we should take steps towards being exemplars for the class that we must organize through developing a ready unity of action. Regardless of comrades' abundant sectarian impulses or doubts, the fact remains that while Karl

Marx was clear about politics being the highest expression of class struggle, he was equally explicit that communists should not see themselves as separate from the movements of proletarians.

In the United States, the long-standing decline of organized labor along with our increasingly corrupt politics has seen Democrats cater almost exclusively to the interests of capital at the cost of working-class voters and their objective interests. While the traditional two-party system of American politics has successfully branded itself as an insurmountable part of how politics here are done, there are many curious facets to this system which expose its vulnerability. American political parties function like ad hoc fundraising committees, formed by rival swarms of established politicians and public figures, and less so like traditional parties that charge dues to members, build up party infrastructure and have well-developed full-time organizational capacity.

The populist and social-democratic campaign of Bernie Sanders had twenty-three organizing offices in California (compared to Joe Biden's three) and won that presidential primary state contest. Funded by an unprecedented number of overwhelmingly working-class donors giving small amounts, the campaign built up a sizable infrastructure. The question of course is this: what happens to all that energy, experience, and infrastructure now that Sanders has been elbowed out of the Democratic primary once again? This is a question we need to be ready to answer if we do not want the movement to lose out to feelings of defeat and despair. Even though the Sanders campaign unified and mobilized millions of people to fight for a society based on the working class's principle of solidarity, there are only so many defeats and dead ends people will be able to tolerate without losing morale.

While voter turn-out among young and poor people in fact rose, albeit not as much as desired, there is a great deal of justified apathy towards voting in this country. Despite an undeniable resurgence of the working class as an actor in the electoral arena, widespread political corruption abounds, with thousands of polling stations in working-class and minority neighborhoods being closed, voters waiting in line for five or more hours to vote, voter purge lists getting rid of millions of cast ballots, mass cancellations of voters' registrations, rigged computer voting systems, disputed vote counts, the caucus recount debacle in the Iowa Democratic Party, and so on. And this is not to mention the coordinated campaign by the corporate media and the Democratic establishment to stop the "socialist Sanders." All these are examples of why there has been good reason for socialists to not share the unbounded electoral enthusiasm some comrades have had. As the Electoral Integrity Project from Harvard reported three years ago, out of the 28 states that had exit polling in the 2016 election, a whopping 25 of them had exit-poll differences outside of the margin of error from the final result in the primary, and 19 of them in the general election. Thus, according to the US government's own standards for evaluating other countries' electoral integrity, 89% of our primary and 68% of our general elections were fraudulent.

Reports of voter suppression in, as well as exit poll data from the 2020 elections definitely suggest that this trend has increased.[ii] As the investigative reporter Greg Palast has put it, in the United States of America you have the right to vote, just not the right to have it counted

All this is not to say that the political situation is hopeless; quite the contrary. Independent leftist media is steadily growing. Bernie Sanders and his campaign have helped to embolden millions of workers and borrowed admirably from the moral legacy of the civil rights movement of the 1960s. With the "democratic road to socialism" barred once more through blatantly undemocratic means, one can hope that campaigns of civil disobedience to fight for electoral and other reforms will eventually take root. This was, incidentally, one of Kautsky's conceptions of what shape a proletarian revolution would take. But politics and democracy, however much the American ruling class would have us believe the contrary, are not simply played out on the electoral front. For revolutionary parties, electoral politics serves primarily as a tool of propaganda and an indicator of relative strength. While the Republican Donald Trump and Democrat Joe Biden nominally have widespread support, the status quo and decrepit system they champion is built on a marshy foundation; their support is a very superficial one, not based on a programmatic, close, and collaborative relationship between a committed mass membership and elected representatives of a party, but rather on the support of hypocritical individualists and those public figures that the corporate media tell us "matter."

In opposition to this dreary morass of decadence and overwhelming corruption there must develop not only a movement that expresses the righteous anger of the untold billions of oppressed from all around the world, but a mass socialist party-movement. Besides organizing the working class, we should as well strive to inspire the diverse movements for justice with the certainty of scientific socialism and clarify the historical conditions under and for which humanity is struggling. Whereas some socialists today advocate for a third type of party that aims to govern effectively (over the bourgeois state), gaining trust from the working class is not done by electing esteemed senators, honorable judges of our own, nor by sowing further illusions in bourgeois politics, but by throwing off the cloak of bourgeois society, organizing and fighting side by side with the working class, shop floor by shop floor, community by community. We must be honest with the people whom we seek to bring into the movement for the future, honest and clear about our ultimate aims and the sacrifices entailed if we are to win the struggle against barbarism. The isolated struggles of all workers must become our own, and the struggle of humanity consciously become the cause of all workers. Most importantly, and most difficult for many, we must not bend or kowtow to reactionary attitudes we face in the working class, but face its diverse and sometimes hostile attitudes to socialism with an open mind, yet unshakeable faith in the righteousness of the cause of labor and in its ultimate triumph over ignorance and division.

We have to struggle assuredly for the unity of the class, readying it for collective action and international solidarity.

In order for the working class to effectively build such solidarity, it cannot be restrained or corrupted by the always extant yellow or right-wing trade unionist bureaucrats, as it more often than not is. The working class's most advanced leaders and organizers should, however, also not fall prey to shortcuts to winning the working class to its objective class interest: socialism. Nice-sounding slogans, radical demands, and demonstrative actions of activist "grassroots campaigns," regardless of the amount of individual activist labor invested in them, historically do little to challenge the most common power relations within unions or actually advance the communist program within them. What is in fact effective and needed is the development of left programmatic unity and consequently a conscious and *concerted effort* by the left in *large numbers* to enter the labor movement, fight for the program in the working class, and attain the financial means to build a mass-media apparatus.

As Kautsky explains in an important explication of his Erfurt Program, it is the duty of Marxists not only to labor to bring about the political unity of socialism with the workers' movement as outlined in *The Historic Accomplishment of Karl Marx*, but furthermore to advance the struggle for democratic rights in broader society and to "build a state within a state."[iii] While he elaborates on the social democratic demand to replace the bourgeoisie's standing armies with a people's militia, it is true that

Kautsky throughout does not explicitly point towards a violent confrontation between this rising socialist party-movement and the state; yet this does not make him less radical today. Kautsky's strategy of patiently building a proletarian opposition and his revolutionary writings are of lasting importance because they are altogether much more resolute, congruent, and informed by a lucid wisdom than one usually sees on the left today. Under the conditions of "civilized" bourgeois democracy, it is clearly much more productive, far-sighted, and actually revolutionary to build a principled, civil, mass opposition — one that exploits all possible legal means to grow its power, which seeks to challenge bourgeois authority and culture in all corners of society — than it is to dream of theoretical communist utopias and spontaneous revolutions to bring them about. This political struggle to challenge bourgeois authority must not only be a challenge to the legitimacy of the institutions of capitalism and its servants, but a challenge *for* the legitimacy of our own democratic institutions and party, our state within the state. It goes without saying that if the narrow confines of bourgeois law continue to not only demonstrate their inability to address the growing injustices of capitalism, but actually enhance them and criminalize the inevitable and *necessary* proletarian rebellions against this order, a socialist adherence to strict legality will meet its limits.

The acutely predictable catastrophic possibilities of our world today, of an apparently unstoppable climate change spurring on the development of ever more diseases, a deep economic depression, and the collection of social crises that are on display in the "advanced" capitalist societies — from income inequality, corruption, racism, the brutal carceral state, to sexism and more — nonetheless hang like a dark, stifling cloud over the heads of all who possess even an ounce of critical thought. The collection of crises needing to be fixed will not disappear any time soon. It appears to many that we live in a time when the world is in fact rushing towards mass extinction and humanity is lost. Every once in a while, however, history's unusual circumstances bring forward movements and individuals who redeem confidence in humanity's ability to acclaim a better and more egalitarian future. To Kautsky, it is clear that Karl Marx was such an individual.

Sharing this previously untranslated work with the English-speaking world has, to the translator, much more purpose than just another simple academic exercise. The leftist "common wisdom" on Karl Kautsky is one that overlooks Kautsky's insight and revolutionary work quite unanimously, to our detriment, as in part IV, the "Summary of German, French, and English Thought," where Kautsky gives a glimpse of his opinion on what should be socialists' attitude towards the armies of the bourgeoisie: sabotage. Quite in contrast to pacifism, he goes on to speak positively of the historical "combativeness" of the Parisians, who repeatedly won concessions from the ruling classes through armed insurrection. Without a doubt, Kautsky read and understood Marx's lessons from the defeated Paris Commune and, despite the stranglehold of the German censors, must have understood the pinnacle of proletarian organization as necessarily being a centralized government and a fighting force, an army.

While the political situation in the United States was until recently far from one that could be described as a national or revolutionary crisis, the powers that be are not as short-sighted as they often appear. US intelligence services and the Pentagon, for instance, are very aware of the mortal danger that primarily climate change (with its induction of more disease, weather volatility, and indeed famine) can and might spell for US society and its state. If Kautsky was pointing out the French and German armies' vulnerability to sabotage in 1908, what word would one use to characterize the armies of today? Endangered? Military scholars are more than concerned about the defenselessness of expensive modern armies in wars against relatively low budget combatants. The Houthis have claimed that their drone attacks against Saudi Arabia in 2019, which caused 5% of the world's oil supply to fall for almost a month, amounted to hundreds of millions of dollars in damages for the Saudi royal family, damages caused by drones which likely only cost a few tens of thousands of dollars. The reliance on electricity by modern countries and armies for almost everything is the biggest vulnerability, as it is nearly impossible to adequately protect an electrical grid or store the amount of electricity necessary to power a nation with today's batteries.

What is clear in these times is that if we want to save humanity from the depths of chaos and a total collapse of civilization, we have to strive for the most rigorous theory that can hold up against our urgent need for practice and build the seeds of a mass proletarian democracy in the shell of class society. Early German Social-Democracy, although it had organizational flaws of its own, stands as a prime example of building a mass Marxist opposition party and proletarian alternative culture. Whereas Kautsky tirelessly defended Marxist orthodoxy, his systematization of the doctrine and "orthodoxy" was not one which betrayed his own intellect nor denied freedom of debate; quite the opposite. Despite widespread accusations of dogmatism, fanaticism, and every other possible absurdity, orthodox Marxism found in its stride many fellow travelers and flourished. A wide variety of socialists regularly published their thoughts in *Die Neue Zeit* and were allowed to express theoretical challenges, from Austria's Otto Bauer, Russia's Alexander Bogdanov and Leon Trotsky, to even Kautsky's rival Eduard Bernstein. In his own right, Kautsky possessed a lively intellectual interest and continuously analyzed new scientific findings and social developments through the lens of historical materialism.

Clearly recognizable throughout this work and others is the foundational influence of Kautsky's thought and defense of Marxist orthodoxy against revisionism. Specific words, concepts, and idiosyncrasies that he formulated in his lifelong fight to clarify and defend Marxism breached through history into the future and were picked up by official Communism. The central use of his locutions in the twentieth and twenty-first centuries by a slew of subsequent Marxist tendencies must be seen in the light of the origins of Marxism as a developing mass phenomenon; without Karl Kautsky's founding and editorship of the SPD's legendary weekly *Die Neue Zeit*, it would be difficult to speculate on this phenomenon. As a number of historians such as Moira Donald and Lars Lih have demonstrated, Kautsky's thought and tremendous work was vital in the formation of Marxism and the greatest Marxist revolution of human history as of yet: October 1917.

— *Alexander Gallus*

---

[i] https://splinternews.com/afl-cio-budget-is-a-stark-illustration-of-the-decline-o-1834793722/

[ii] https://www.electoralintegrityproject.com/eip-blogs/2017/1/7/its-even-worse-than-the-news-about-north-carolina-american-elections-rank-last-among-all-western-democracies/
http://tdmsresearch.com/2020/03/04/massachusetts-2020-democratic-party-primary/

[iii] Kautksy, Grundsätze und Forderungen Der Sozialdemokratie, 38.

A Note on the Translation

Kautsky infamously reneged on the principles for which he had fought for decades and as laid out in his 1908 *The Historic Accomplishment of Karl Marx*. He noted in a foreword to the 1933 third edition, originally used to translate this piece, that it was "published unchanged, with only a few timely allusions." The translator has seen fit to restore to the original edition or remove certain, in our opinion, *un*timely allusions in a very few passages, mostly pertaining to the accuracy of dates or subtle remarks about the Bolshevik revolution.

When translating this piece, the word "Geist," among others, was one which frequently posed a dilemma: both the words "intellect" and "spirit" are common translations. Kautsky's frequent use of the word "Geist" when speaking of Marx leaves room open for interpretation. We the editors have often opted for using the words "intellect" and "intellectual."

What is clear, however, is that Marx was a person not only of great thought but also of great feeling. Instead of being uncomfortable with the often-adulatory treatment of Marx as an individual, we should recognize that Marx was an outstandingly dedicated and talented fighter worthy of celebration. His theoretical and practical work undoubtedly changed how billions of people thought and changed history. We should find comfort that our tireless work for the communist future of humanity shall be recognized by future generations as well. There is no labor greater than that which gives without a thought of personal remuneration and knows its eventual yield to be measured in values far greater than dollars and cents.

— *AG*

On behalf of the Bremen Education Committee, I gave a lecture on Karl Marx in Bremen on the 17th of December last year. Comrades from Bremen who heard the lecture asked me to publish it in print, because it was suitable for correcting widespread misconceptions about what Marx had achieved and what Marxism means. I hereby comply with this request, but I do not limit myself to a mere rendition of the lecture. I have extended it several times for print, namely in its first part. What I am giving here is not a eulogy for Karl Marx. It would not suit the sensibility of the man whose motto was: follow your own path and let people talk. It would as well be tasteless at a time when his personal significance is recognized by the whole world. Rather, the point here is to make it easier to understand what Marx brought to the world. This is unfortunately not as well known as it is necessary in a period in which Marx is the subject of much debate, for and against. Some may discover while reading these pages that these thoughts, which have become a matter of course today, were developed through laborious work. But they will also find that ideas which are praised today as surprising new discoveries, through which "outdated" Marxism is supposed to be overcome or educated, basically represent nothing more than the revival of views and ways of thinking which were rampant before Marx, and which were worn down and overcome precisely by Marx, but which appear again and again before new generations for whom the past of our movement is foreign. Therefore, the present work is not only intended to be a study of party history, but also a contribution to decisions on current issues.

Friedenau, February 1908

K. Kautsky

I
Introduction

On the 14th of March, 1908, it will have been 25 years since Karl Marx died, and at the start of the same year it had been 60 years since *The Communist Manifesto* first appeared, in which his new doctrine found its first fulfilled expression. Those are long time spans for such a fast-paced period like ours, which changes its scientific and artistic views as quickly as its trends. Karl Marx still lives among us in full vigor, and he dominates the thought of our time more than ever, despite all crises of Marxism, despite all refutations and enlightened conquests from the podiums of bourgeois science.

This surprising and constantly growing influence would be a mystery were it not for Marx's success in bringing to light the deepest roots of capitalist society. Having done that, then naturally, so long as that social form endures, new social discoveries of any weighty significance are not to be found beyond Marx, and hence the path he indicated remains much more theoretically and practically fruitful than any other. The powerful and enduring influence of Marx on modern thought would however also be unreasonable were it not for his endeavor to run past, in spirit and mind, the confines of the capitalist process of production. His recognition of capitalism's intrinsic tendencies which point toward a higher social order prompted him to point out yet-distant goals. Through unfolding development, these goals become ever nearer and within reach of mankind, who grasps them with clarity to the same degree it becomes aware of its own greatness.

It is this unique combination of scientific depth and revolutionary daring that has led us to the fact that Karl Marx today, half a century after his death and almost three generations since his first appearance on the public stage, has greater influence today than when he was alive.

If one attempts to understand the nature of the historical achievement of this marvelous man, one can perhaps summarize it best by realizing the breadth of his work, combining biology with the humanities, merging English, French, and German philosophy, as well as the workers' movement and socialism, in both theory and practice. That he succeeded without parallel in not only knowing these various fields of study, but in mastering them, made it possible for Karl Marx to accomplish the historic feat of having his character stamped on the late decades of the nineteenth century, and the twentieth century.

II
Summary of Natural Science and the Humanities

The foundation for all of Karl Marx's lasting success is his theoretical rigor. This we have to be most aware of. But it is this fact that presents itself as a challenge for a popular presentation [of Marxism]. We will hopefully overcome this dilemma in spite of limited intimations or clues. In any case, the points covered after this one will be easy to understand. The reader should not shy from plowing through the next few pages to get to these latter points.

The sciences are divided into two great categories: the natural sciences, which research the dynamics of living and non-living objects and the humanities, which are unjustly named such; only if the subject of study in humanities takes the form of one single individual is it given attention. The field of psychology, stemming from the humanities, operates solely with the methods of natural science without ever considering curing the spiritual illness plaguing humanity. The narrow application of natural science in this field unfortunately remains unrivaled.

What is called "the humanities" is in reality a social science, a science which analyzes man's relation to his fellow men. Only certain relationships are eligible, however, and only some intellectual expressions in human society come into consideration and are examined by the humanities.

Within the humanities themselves two groups can be distinguished.: The first is those which study human society as such, or man as he exists en masse. These include: political economy, the study of the laws of the social economy under the rules of commodity production; ethnology, the study of social conditions in all their tribal diversity; and, finally, prehistory, the study of social conditions from that time before written witness.

The other group of the humanities comprises sciences which up to now have primarily emanated from the individual and dealt with the position and effect of the individual in and on society: history, jurisprudence, and ethics or morality.

This second group of humanities is ancient and has always had the greatest influence on human thought. The first group, on the other hand, developed at the time of Marx's youth and had only just arrived at scientific methods. It remained restricted to specialists and had no influence on general thinking, which was influenced by the natural sciences and the humanities of the second group.

There was then a huge gap between the latter two types of sciences, which was revealed in contemporary worldviews.

Natural science had uncovered so many necessary, legitimate connections and laws in nature;

that is, it had repeatedly tested the identification of cause with effect so that it thoroughly incorporated the assumption of general lawfulness in nature. It therefore completely banished from its practice the assumption of mysterious powers which mythically intervene in natural events at will. Modern man no longer seeks to make such powers favorable to himself through prayers and sacrifices, but only to recognize the lawful connections in nature in order to be able to achieve in it, through his intervention, those effects which he needs for his existence or comfort.

This is not the case in the humanities. These were still dominated by the assumption of the freedom of the human will, which was not subject to any such lawful necessity. The jurists and ethicists felt urged to hold on to this assumption, because otherwise they would lose the ground under their feet. If man is a product of circumstances, if his actions and will have the necessary effect of causes that do not depend on his own will, what should become of sin and punishment, of good and evil, of legal and moral condemnation?

The motive of that accusation was of course only a motive of "practical reason," not logical reasoning from proof. These practical reasons were provided primarily by historical science, which was essentially based on nothing other than the collection of written documents from earlier times, in which the acts of some individuals, namely the rulers, were communicated either by themselves or by others. It seemed impossible to discover any inherent necessary laws behind these individual acts. In vain did scientific thinkers try to find such laws. They were, however, reluctant to accept that the general laws of nature should not apply to man's actions.

Experience offered them enough material to show that the human mind was no exception in nature, that it always responded to certain causes with certain effects. However, as undeniable as this could be for the simpler activities which man has in common with animals, for his complicated activities, for social ideas and ideals, the natural scientists could not find the necessary causal connections. They could not fill this gap. They could claim that the human spirit was only a part of nature and within its necessary context, but they could not prove it sufficiently in all areas. Their materialistic monism remained incomplete and could not break with idealism and dualism.

Then Marx came and saw that the history, ideas, and ideals of man, and their successes and failures, are the result of class struggles. But he saw even more. Class antagonisms and class struggles had already been seen before him in history, but they had mostly appeared as the work of stupidity and malice on the one hand, of arrogance and enlightenment on the other; only Marx uncovered their necessary connection with economic conditions, the laws of which had been laid down by the laws of time. These economic conditions themselves, however, are again ultimately based on nature and the extent of man's domination of nature, which emerges from the knowledge of its laws.

Only under certain social conditions is the driving force of history the class struggle; it is always ultimately the struggle against nature. No matter how peculiar human society may seem to the rest of nature, here and there we find the same kind of movement and development through the struggle of opposites that emerge again and again from nature itself: dialectical development.

Thus, social development was placed within the framework of natural development, the human spirit presented as a part of nature, even in its most complicated and supreme manifestations. The natural laws of social development were hence proven in all fields and the last ground taken away from philosophical idealism and dualism.

In this way, Marx not only completely revolutionized the science of history, but also filled the gap between the natural sciences and the humanities, established the unity of all human science, and thus made philosophy superfluous, insofar as philosophy, as a special wisdom outside and above the sciences, sought to establish a unified thought about the world process which could not previously be gained from the sciences.

It means a tremendous *elevation*[*] of science, which Marx brought about with his conception of history; the entirety of human thought and understanding had to be fertilized in the most powerful way — but strangely, bourgeois science was completely hostile to it. Only in opposition to bourgeois science, as a special, proletarian science, could this new scientific conception prevail.

The opposition between bourgeois and proletarian science was mocked, as if there could be bourgeois and proletarian chemistry or mathematics!

---

[*] Emphasis added — Trans.

But the mockers only prove that they do not know what it is.

Marx's discovery of the materialistic conception of history had two preconditions. One was a certain raising of scientific development, the other a revolutionary point of view.

The laws of historical development could only be recognized when the new humanities — political economy, economic history, then ethnology and prehistory — had reached a certain height. Only these sciences, from whose material the individual was excluded from the outset, and which were based on mass observations, could reveal the basic laws of social development and thus pave the way for the investigation of those trends which propel individuals to the surface appearance and who alone observe and record the conventional representation of history.

These new humanities developed first with the capitalist mode of production and its international trade, and could only really achieve significant gains when capital had come to rule; but soon the bourgeoisie had ceased to be a revolutionary class.

Only a revolutionary class, however, was able to accept the doctrine of class struggle. A class that wants to conquer power in society must also want the struggle for power; it will easily understand its necessity. A class which has power will regard every opposing struggle for it as an unwelcome disturbance and will reject any doctrine which demonstrates its necessity. It will appear all the more against it if the doctrine of class struggle is a doctrine of social development which, as a necessary conclusion of the present class struggle, sets forth the overthrow of the present masters of society.

But the teaching that people are the products of social conditions, to the extent that the members of a particular social form differ from the people of other social forms, is also not acceptable to a conservative class, because the only way to change people consequently then is to change society itself. As long as the bourgeoisie was revolutionary, it also paid homage to the view that people were the products of society, but unfortunately, at that time, the sciences with which the driving forces of social development could have been recognized were not yet sufficiently developed. The French materialists of the eighteenth century did not know the class struggle and did not pay attention to technical development. They knew that in order to change people one had to change society, but they did not know where the forces that would change society would come from. They saw it in the omnipotence of individual extraordinary men, especially schoolmasters. Beyond that, bourgeois materialism did not develop.

As soon as the bourgeoisie became conservative, it found the thought intolerable that it was the social conditions that were to blame for the particular grievances of their time and that they had to be changed. As far as it thinks scientifically, the bourgeoisie now seeks to prove that men are and must be as they are because of nature, that wanting to change society means nothing more than turning the natural order upside down. One must, however, have been educated very exclusively in natural science and have remained unaffected by the social conditions of our time in order to assert its necessary natural continuity for all time. The majority of the bourgeoisie no longer finds the courage even for this, seeking consolation by denying materialism and recognizing freedom of the will. It is not society that makes people, they assert, but rather people who make society according to their will. It is imperfect because they are. We must improve society not by social transformations, but by raising the individual higher, by instilling in them a higher morality. The better people will then surely produce a better society. In this way, ethics and the recognition of the freedom of the will become the favorite doctrine of today's bourgeoisie. It is supposed to show the good will of the bourgeoisie to counteract social grievances and yet not commit it to any societal change, but on the contrary, to repel any such change.

From this perspective, the insights that can be gained from the basis of the unity of all the sciences, as developed by Marx, are inaccessible to anyone who stands on the ground of bourgeois society. Only those who are critical of the existing society can grasp these insights, that is, only those who stand on the ground of the proletariat. In this respect one can distinguish between proletarian and bourgeois science.

Of course, the contrast between the two is most pronounced in the humanities, while the contrast between feudal or Catholic and bourgeois science is most pronounced in the natural sciences. But man's thinking always strives for uniformity, as the various fields of knowledge always influence each other, and therefore our social perceptions affect our entire conception of the world. Thus, the contrast between bourgeois and proletarian science is also reflected in the natural sciences.

This can already be seen in Greek philosophy, as shown, among other things, by an example from modern natural science which is closely related to our subject. I have already pointed out in another place that the bourgeoisie, as long as it was revolutionary, also assumed that natural development took place through catastrophes. Ever since it became conservative, it has not wanted to know anything about catastrophes in nature either. In its opinion, development is now taking place very slowly, exclusively by means of imperceptible changes. Catastrophes appear to it to be something abnormal, unnatural, only capable of disrupting natural development. And despite Darwin's doctrine of the struggle for existence, bourgeois science does its utmost to make the concept of evolutionary development appear synonymous with that of a completely peaceful process.

For Marx, on the other hand, the class struggle was only a special form of nature's general law of development, which is by no means peaceful. For him, development, as we have already noted, is "dialectical," that is, the product of a struggle of opposites that necessarily occur. Every fight of irreconcilable opposites, however, must ultimately lead to the overcoming of one of the fighters: that is, to a catastrophe. The catastrophe can prepare itself very slowly; imperceptibly the strength of one fighter may grow, that of the other absolutely or proportionally diminish, until finally the collapse of one part becomes inevitable — that is, inevitable as a result of the fight and the increase of the strength of one part, not inevitable as an event that takes place by itself. Every day, at every turn, we encounter small catastrophes, both in nature and in society. Every death is a catastrophe. Every existing structure must eventually succumb to a supremacy of opposites. This applies not only to plants and animals, but also to whole societies, whole kingdoms, entire celestial bodies. For them, too, the progress of the general development process prepares temporary catastrophes through the gradual increase of resistance. No movement and no development without temporary catastrophes are possible. These form a necessary stage of development, since evolution is impossible without temporary revolutions.

By this conception, we also find the revolutionary bourgeois one overcome, which assumed that development takes place *exclusively* through catastrophes. The conservative bourgeois revolution thereafter [in contrast to the proletarian one] saw in catastrophe not the necessary point of passage of an often quite slow and imperceptible development process, but a disturbance and inhibition of this process.

We find another contrast between bourgeois and proletarian, or if we prefer, between conservative and revolutionary science, in the critique of knowledge: a revolutionary class that feels the power within itself to conquer society is not inclined to recognize any barrier to its scientific conquests and feels itself capable of solving all the problems of its time. A conservative class, on the other hand, instinctively shuns any progress not only in the political and social fields, but also in the scientific field, because it feels that any deeper knowledge can no longer be of much use to it, but can harm it infinitely. It is inclined to reduce confidence in science.

The naive confidence that still animated the revolutionary thinkers of the eighteenth century, as if they were carrying the solution to all world riddles in their pockets, as if they were speaking in the name of absolute reason, can no longer be shared even by the boldest revolutionary today. Today no one will want to deny anymore what, of course, already in the eighteenth century, and even in antiquity, some thinkers knew, namely that all our knowledge is relative; that it represents a relationship of man, of the self, to the rest of the world, and shows us only this relationship, not the world itself. So all knowledge is relative, conditioned, and limited; there are no absolute, eternal truths. But this means nothing other than that there is no conclusion to our knowledge, that the process of knowledge is an infinite, unlimited one, that it is foolish to present any knowledge as the ultimate conclusion of truth, but no less foolish to present any proposition as the ultimate limit of wisdom, beyond which we could never get.

Rather, we know that mankind has still succeeded in crossing every limit of its knowledge of which it became aware sooner or later, of course only to find further limits behind it of which it previously had no idea. We have not the least reason to shy away from any particular problem that we are able to recognize nor to let our hands sink into our laps and mumble resignedly: *ignorabimus*, we will never know anything about it. But this despondency characterizes modern bourgeois thinking. Instead of striving with all its might to broaden and deepen our knowledge, today it spends its noblest power on finding out certain limits that should be drawn from our knowledge forever and discrediting the certainty of scientific knowledge.

When the bourgeoisie was revolutionary, it avoided such tasks. For this despondency Marx never had anything to spare, much to the indignation of today's bourgeois philosophy.

III
Marx and Engels

It was his revolutionary, proletarian standpoint that allowed an intellectual giant like Marx to establish the unity of all science. But when we speak of Marx, we must never forget that the same feat was achieved at the same time by an equal thinker, Friedrich Engels, and that without the intimate cooperation of the two, the new materialistic conception of history and the new historical or dialectical conception of the world could not have appeared so completely and comprehensively in one fell swoop.

Engels arrived at this view by other means than Marx. Marx was the son of a lawyer, first intended for a legal career, then for an academic one. He studied law, philosophy, and history, and only turned to economic studies when he bitterly felt a lack of economic knowledge.

He studied economics, revolutionary history, and socialism in Paris, and the great thinker Saint-Simon seems to have had a great influence on him. These studies then led him to the realization that it was not the law, nor the state, which makes society, but vice versa, that the society arising from the economic process makes the law, the state, according to its need.

Engels, on the other hand, was born the son of a factory owner, and it was not college but a lowlier secondary school that gave him the first foundations of his knowledge; there he learned to think scientifically. Then he became a practical businessman, ran economics practically and theoretically, in England, in Manchester, the center of English capitalism, where his father owned a factory. Familiar with Hegelian philosophy from Germany, he knew how to deepen the economic knowledge he had gained in England, and his gaze was directed above all to economic history. But nowhere in the forties of the nineteenth century was the proletarian class struggle so developed and its connection with capitalist development as clear as in England.

Thus, Engels arrived at the same time as Marx, yet in a different way, at the threshold of the same materialistic conception of history. One arrived at this via the old humanities, jurisprudence, ethics, and history, the other via the new economy, economic history, ethnologies, and the natural sciences. In the revolution, and in socialism, they met. The agreement of their ideas was what first brought them closer to each other when they came into personal contact in 1844 in Paris. But the convergence of ideas soon became a complete fusion in a higher unity, in which it is impossible to say what and how much one or the other contributed to it. It is true that Marx was the more important of the two, and no one acknowledged this more enviously, or joyfully, than

Engels himself. Their thought, named Marxism, was also named after Marx. But Marx could never have achieved what he did without Engels, from whom he learnt a great deal, and of course vice versa.

Each of the two was lifted up by the interaction with the other and thus attained a breadth of vision and a universality that he could not have achieved on his own. Marx would have come to the materialistic conception of history even without Engels, Engels also without Marx, but their development would probably have been slower, going through more errors and failures. Marx was the deeper thinker, Engels the bolder. With Marx, the power of theoretical abstraction was more strongly developed, a gift for discovering the general in the confusing abundance of particular phenomena; with Engels, the gift of practical combination, the ability to produce a totality from individual characteristics. Marx's critical faculty was more powerful, as was his self-criticism, which bridled the audacity of his thinking and urged it to cautious progress and constant examination of the ground, while Engels's spirit was easily inspired and flew over the greatest difficulties by the proud joy of the tremendous insights it gained.

Among the many stimuli that Marx received from Engels, one above all has become significant. Marx was greatly elevated by overcoming the one-sided German way of thinking and by fertilizing German thinking with French thinking. Engels also made him familiar with the English spirit. It was only in this way that his thinking achieved the highest upswing possible under the given circumstances. Nothing is more erroneous than declaring Marxism to be a purely German product. It was international from its beginning.

IV
Summary of German, French, and English Thought

Three nations were the victors of modern culture in the nineteenth century. Only he who had filled himself with the spirit of all three, mastered the achievements of all three, was armed with all the achievements of his century; only he was able to achieve the greatest that could be achieved with the means of this century.

The combination of the thinking of these three nations into a higher unity, in which each of their one-sidedness was abolished, forms the starting point of the historical achievement of Marx and Engels.

England, as already mentioned, had developed capitalism further than any other country in the first half of the nineteenth century, mainly thanks to its geographical position, which in the eighteenth century enabled it to take considerable advantage of the colonial policy of conquest and plunder and bled to death those countries of mainland Europe without access to the Atlantic Ocean. Thanks to England's insular position, it did not need to maintain a strong standing army; it could turn all its strength to fleets and gain naval supremacy without exhaustion. Its wealth of coal and iron then allowed it to use the wealth gained through colonial policy to develop a large capitalist industry which, by controlling the sea, reconquered the world market, which in turn could only be exploited for mass consumer goods by water before the development of the railway system.

Earlier than elsewhere, therefore, one could study capitalism and its tendencies in England, but also, as already mentioned, the proletarian class struggle that these tendencies evoked. Nowhere was the recognition of the laws of capitalist production, i.e. political economy, more advanced than in England, thanks to world trade, economic history, and ethnology. Better than anywhere else, one could see in England what the coming period contained in its lap. Yet also, thanks to the new humanities, one could now recognize the laws that dominated the social development of all time, and thus establish the unity of natural science and the humanities.

But England offered only the best material, not the best research methods.

It was precisely because capitalism developed earlier in England than elsewhere that the bourgeoisie came to rule society there, after feudalism had become politically, economically, and spiritually completely deprived and the bourgeoisie had achieved complete independence in every respect. The colonial policy itself, however, which facilitated capitalism, also gave new strength to the feudal lords.

In addition, for the reasons already mentioned, the standing army did not reach a strong development in England. This again prevented the emergence of a strong, central power of government. The bureaucracy remained weak, and the self-government of the ruling classes remained strong alongside it. This meant, however, that the class struggles were not centralized much and were often fragmented.

All this caused the spirit of compromise between old and new to permeate all life and thought. The thinkers and pioneers of the up-and-coming classes did not in principle turn against Christianity, the aristocracy, the monarchy; their parties did not set up any great programs. They did not seek to think their thoughts through to the end; they preferred to defend only certain individual measures which were practically necessary at the time instead of sweeping programs. Limitation and conservatism, overestimation of detail in politics and science, rejection of any aspirations to conquer a great horizon permeated all classes.

Meanwhile the situation in France was quite different. This country was economically much more backward, its capitalist industries dominated by luxury industries and the petty bourgeoisie. The tone was set by the petty bourgeoisie in its big cities like Paris, and such big cities, with half a million inhabitants or more, were few until the introduction of the railways, and they played a very different role than they do today. The armies could only be small before the advent of the railways, which enabled rapid mass transport. They were scattered throughout the country, not quick to assemble, their equipment not as defenseless to the masses as it is today. It was the Parisians in particular who had always distinguished themselves by their distinctive combativeness, long before the Great Revolution, by repeatedly wrestling concessions from the government in armed insurrection.

Before the introduction of compulsory schooling, the improvement of the postal system by railways and telegraphs, and the distribution of daily newspapers in the country, however, the intellectual superiority and influence of the metropolitan population over the rest of the country was tremendously great. At that time, social intercourse offered the masses of uneducated people the only opportunity to educate themselves, above all politically, but also artistically, even scientifically. How much greater was this possibility in the big city than in the country towns and villages! Everything that had spirit in France urged Paris to activate and develop it. Everything that was active in Paris was filled with a higher spirit.

And now this critical, cocky, audacious population saw an outrageous collapse of state power and of the ruling classes.

The same causes that inhibited economic development in France promoted the depletion of feudalism and the state. Colonial policy, in particular, cost the state infinite sacrifices, broke its military and financial strength, and accelerated the economic ruin especially of the peasants, but also of the aristocrats. State, nobility, church were politically, morally and, with the exception of the church, also financially bankrupt, but nevertheless knew how to assert their oppressive rule to the extreme, thanks to the violence which the government had centralized in their hands by the standing army and an extensive bureaucracy, and thanks to the complete abolition of any independent organization among the people.

This finally led to that colossal catastrophe which we know as the great French Revolution, in which at times the petty bourgeois and proletarians of Paris came to dominate all of France, to stand up to all of Europe. But even before that, the increasing sharp contrast between the needs of the masses, led by the liberal bourgeoisie, and those of the aristocrats and the clergy, protected by the power of the state, led to the most radical overthrow of all existing thought. War was declared against all traditional authority. Materialism and atheism, in England mere luxury hobbies of a degenerate nobility (which quickly disappeared with the victory of the bourgeoisie), became in France the way of thinking of the boldest reformers from the aspiring classes.

Nowhere else has the economic root of class antagonisms and class struggles become so evident as in England; nowhere else has it been so clear as in the France of the Great Revolution that all class struggle is a struggle for political power, that the task of every great political party is not limited to one reform or another, but must always bear in mind the conquest of political power, and that this conquest, when carried out by a class which has hitherto been subjugated, always entails a change in the entire social transmission.[†] In the first half of the nineteenth century, economic thinking was most developed in England, while political thinking was most developed in France. While England was dominated by the spirit of compromise, France was dominated by radicalism; in England, the meticulous work of slow organizational development flourished; in France, it was the revolutionary passion which swept everything along with it.

The radical, bold action was preceded by radical, bold thinking which held nothing as sacred, which intrepidly and ruthlessly pursued every knowledge to its final consequences, thought every thought through to its end.

But as brilliant and enchanting as the results of this thought and action were, it also developed the errors of its merits. Full of impatience, it did not take the time to prepare them to reach their ultimate goals. Full of zeal to storm the fortress of the state with revolutionary *élan*, it failed to prepare the organizational ground for its siege. And the urge to advance to the final and supreme truths easily led to the most hasty conclusions from wholly inadequate foundations, replacing patient research with the pleasure of ingenious, spontaneous ideas. An addiction grew to mastering the infinite fullness of life through a few simple formulas and slogans. British sobriety was countered by a Gallic phrase-rush.

[†] Kautsky here means the transmission of an engine: a subjugated class taking power always entails a radical shift in the way the "engine" of society distributes power — Trans.

Yet the situation in Germany was different again.

There capitalism had developed far less than in France because it was almost completely cut off from the great road of world trade in Europe, the Atlantic Ocean, and therefore recovered only slowly from the horrific devastation of the Thirty Years' War. Much more than France, Germany was a petty-bourgeois country, but at the same time was a country without a strong central state power. Fragmented into innumerable small states, it had no great capital; small states and small towns made its petty bourgeoisie limited, weak, and cowardly. The ultimate collapse of feudalism was not brought about by an uprising from within, but by an invasion from without. Not German citizens, but French soldiers swept it out of the most important parts of Germany.

The great successes of the rising bourgeoisie in England and France probably also excited the German bourgeoisie. But, to the determination of the most energetic and intelligent of its members, each of the territories conquered by the bourgeoisie of Western Europe remained closed. They could not establish and run large commercial and industrial enterprises, intervene in the fate of the state in parliaments and a powerful press, command fleets or armies. Reality was desolate for them; they had no choice but to turn away from reality in pure thought and to transfigure reality through art. Here they created great things; here the German people surpassed France and England. While they produced a Pitt, Fox and Burke, Mirabeau, Danton, Robespierre, Nelson and Napoleon, Germany produced a Schiller, Goethe, Kant, Fichte, and Hegel.

Thinking became the noblest occupation of the great Germans, the idea became the ruler of the world for them, the revolution of thought the means to revolutionize the world. The more miserable and limited reality was, the more thought sought to rise above it, to overcome its barriers, to grasp the entire infinity.

While the English devised the best methods for the triumph of their fleets and industries, the French the best methods for the triumph of their armies and their insurrections, the Germans devised the best methods for the triumph of thought and research.

But this triumphal march, like the French and English, also had its disadvantages in its aftermath, both for theory and practice. The abandonment of reality produced an alienation from the world and an overestimation of the ideas to which life and strength were attributed, independent of the minds of the people who produced them and who had to realize them. One was content with being right in theory and failed to seek power in order to apply that theory. As deep as German philosophy was, as thorough as German science was, as rapturous as German idealism was, as glorious as its creations were, there was unspeakable practical impotence and complete renunciation of any striving for power concealed beneath it. The German ideals were far more illustrious than the French or even the English. But no step was taken to get closer to them. It was stated from the outset that the ideal was the unattainable.

Like English conservatism and the French radical phrase, the Germans' inactive idealism continued for a long time. The industrial development of the great economy finally abolished it, even replacing it with military resolve. In the past, however, Germany found a counter-effect in the invasion of the French spirit after the revolution. Germany owes some of its greatest minds to the mixture of French revolutionary thinking with German philosophical methods — remember only Heinrich Heine and Ferdinand Lassalle.

But the result was even more powerful when this mixture was fertilized with English economic insight. We owe the achievement of Engels and Marx to this.

They recognized how economics and politics, detailed organizational work and revolutionary *Sturm und Drang*, complement each other, how detailed organizational work remains infertile without a great goal in which it finds its constant guideline and its encouragement, and how this goal floats in the air without preparation, which creates only the necessary power for its attainment. They also recognized, however, that such a goal must not be born of a mere revolutionary need, if it is to remain free of illusions and self-intoxication; if it is to be won by the most conscientious application of the methods of scientific research, it must always be in harmony with the total knowledge of mankind. They also recognized that the economy forms the basis of social development, that it contains the laws according to which this development necessarily takes place.

England offered them most of the actual economic material, the philosophy of Germany the best method of deriving from this material the goal of present social development; the revolution of France finally showed them most clearly how we have to gain power, namely political power, to achieve this goal.

Thus, they created modern scientific socialism by uniting into a higher unity all which is great and fruitful in English, French, and German thought.

V

The Merging of the Workers' Movement and Socialism

The materialist conception of history in itself signified a new epoch. It marked the beginning of a new era of science, despite all the resistance of bourgeois scholarship; it defined a new epoch not only in the history of *thought*, but also in the history of the *fight* for social development, of politics in the broadest and highest sense of the word. For it was through it that the workers' movement and socialism were united, thus giving the proletarian class struggle the most potent strength possible.

The workers' movement and socialism are by no means inherently one. The workers' movement is necessarily born as resistance against industrial capitalism wherever it occurs; it expropriates and subjugates the working masses, but also crowds and unites them in large enterprises and industrial cities. The most original form of the workers' movement is the purely economic one, the struggle for wages and working hours, which at first merely takes the form of simple outbursts of despair, of repeatedly unprepared actions, but is soon transformed into higher forms by *trade-union organization*. Early on, the political struggle arose parallel to this. The bourgeoisie itself needed proletarian help in its struggles against feudalism and called for it. The workers soon learned to appreciate the importance of political freedom and political power for their own ends. In England and France in particular, universal suffrage early on became the object of the political aspirations of the proletarians and led to a proletarian party in England in the 1830s, that of the Chartists.

Socialism was already emerging, but by no means in the proletariat. It is certainly, however, like the labor movement, a product of capitalism; with the growth of capitalism, it arises from the urge to counter the misery that capitalist exploitation imposes on the working classes. Meanwhile, the proletariat's self-defense in the form of the labor movement arises wherever a large working-class population gathers, while socialism requires deep insight into the nature of modern society. Every type of socialism is based on the realization that capitalist misery cannot be brought to an end on the ground of bourgeois society, that this misery is based on private ownership of the means of production and will only disappear with it. All socialist systems agree that they deviate from each other only in the ways in which they want to see private property abolished and in the ideas they have about the new social property to replace it.

As naïve as the expectations and proposals of the socialists might sometimes have been, the knowledge on which they were based presupposed a social knowledge that was still completely inaccessible to the proletariat in the first decades of the nineteenth century. Only a man who was able to stand on the ground of the proletariat, to view bourgeois society from its point of view, could come to socialist knowledge. But he could only be one who mastered the means of science, which at that time were still far more accessible to the bourgeois circles than they are today. As naturally and consequently as the workers' movement develops from capitalist production, wherever it reaches a certain height, socialism in its development did not only have capitalism as a prerequisite, but also a confluence of extraordinarily rare circumstances. Everywhere socialism could at first only arise from a bourgeois milieu. In England, even until recently, socialism was propagated primarily by bourgeois elements.

This background appeared as a contradiction to Marx's theory of class struggle, but it would only be such if the *class* of the bourgeoisie had ever adopted socialism somewhere, or if Marx had declared it impossible for individual non-proletarians to accept, for unique reasons, the standpoint of the proletariat.

Marx had always asserted that the only power capable of helping socialism to break through is the working class. In other words, the proletariat can only free itself by its own efforts. But this by no means implies that only proletarians can show it the way.

That socialism is nothing if it is not supported by a strong workers' movement no longer needs proof today. The other side of this coin, that the workers' movement can only unfold its full power if it has understood and accepted socialism, is not so clear today.

Socialism is not the product of an ethic outside of time and space or all class distinctions; it is basically nothing but the science of society from the point of view of the proletariat. But science does not merely serve to satisfy our desire for new things and knowledge of the unknown and the mysterious; it also has an economic purpose, that of sparing energy. It makes it possible for man to navigate reality more easily, to use his powers more expediently, to avoid any useless expenditure of energy, and thus to achieve at all times the maximum of what can be achieved under the given circumstances. At its starting point science directly and consciously serves such purposes of the economization of exertion. The more it develops and moves away from this point of departure, the more mediators come between the activity of its research and its eventual practical effect. But the connection between the two can only be obscured, not broken.

Similarly, the social science of the proletariat, socialism, serves to make possible the most efficient application of exertion and helps it to achieve its highest possible development. Naturally, it achieves this the more, the more perfected it is itself and the deeper its knowledge of reality is.

Socialist theory is by no means the fruitless gimmickry of some parlor scholars, but a very practical thing for the struggling proletariat.

Its main weapon is the concentration of its totality in vast, independent organizations, free from all bourgeois influences. It cannot achieve this without a socialist theory, alone capable of finding out the common proletarian interest among the colorful diversity of the various proletarian strata, and of sharply and permanently separating them altogether from the bourgeois world.

Incapable of this achievement is the naive labor movement, which is bare of any theory, and which rises of its own accord in the working classes against growing capitalism.

Let us examine, for example, the trade unions. They are professional associations that seek to protect the immediate interests of their members. But how different these interests are in the individual professions, how different they are with the seafarers than with the coal diggers, the cab drivers, or the typesetters! Without socialist theory, the individual proletarian professions are not able to recognize the commonality of their interests, are foreign to each other, sometimes even hostile to each other.

Since the trade union only represents the interests of its members, it does not easily stand in opposition to the entire bourgeois world, but initially only to the capitalists of its profession. Besides these capitalists, however, there is now a whole row of bourgeois elements which draw their existence either directly or indirectly from the exploitation of proletarians, who are therefore interested in maintaining the bourgeois social order and who will oppose any attempt to put an end to proletarian exploitation. Whether the spinner of Manchester earns 2 or 2.5 shillings a day, whether he worked 10 or 12 hours a day, a big landowner, a banker, a newspaper owner, or a lawyer would be completely indifferent if they did not own spinning shares. They might have an interest in making certain concessions to the trade unionists in order to win political favors from them. Thus, where trade unions were not enlightened by a socialist theory, they were given the opportunity to serve purposes that were nothing less than "proletarian."[‡]

But even worse could happen and, moreover, did happen. Not all proletarian strata are able to seize trade-union organization. In the proletariat there is a difference between organized and unorganized workers. Where they are filled with socialist thinking, they become the most militant parts of the proletariat, the protagonists of its entirety. Where the organized workers lack this thinking, they become all too easily aristocrats who not only lose all interest in the unorganized workers, but often even oppose them, hindering their organization in order to monopolize its advantages. But the unorganized workers are incapable of any struggle, any ascent, without the help of the organized ones. The more

---

[‡] Kautsky here is playing with the colloquial use of "proletarian" in German to mean something primitive.
— Trans.

they rise, the more they fall into misery without their support. Thus, the trade union movement, despite all the strengthening of individual strata, can even bring about a direct weakening of the entire proletariat if it is not filled with a socialist spirit.

Yet even the political organization of the proletariat cannot develop its full power without this spirit. This is clearly testified to by the first labor party in England, Chartism, born in 1835. This movement contained very far-reaching and far-sighted elements, but in its entirety it did not pursue a specific socialist program, but only individual, practical, easily attainable goals, above all universal suffrage, which of course was not to be an end in itself, but a means to an end; but for the total mass of the Chartists this again consisted only of individual economic demands, above all the ten-hour normal working day.

This first had the disadvantage that the party did not become an unadulterated class party. The general right to vote was also of interest to the petty bourgeoisie.

To some it might seem an advantage for the petty bourgeoisie to join the workers' party as such. But this only makes it more numerous, not stronger. The proletariat has its own interests and its own methods of struggle, which differ from those of all other classes. It is constrained by unity with the others and cannot develop its full power. We Social-Democrats welcome individual petty bourgeois and peasants if they want to join us; but only when they stand on proletarian ground, when they have proletarian feeling. Our socialist program ensures that only such petty-bourgeois and smallholder elements come to us. The Chartists lacked such a program, and so their electoral struggle was joined by numerous petty-bourgeois elements who had as little sympathy as they had inclination for the proletarian interests and methods of struggle. The natural consequence was thriving internal conflict within Chartism, which weakened it greatly.

The defeat of the 1848 revolution then put an end to all political workers' movement for a decade. When the European proletariat stirred up again, the struggle for universal suffrage began anew in the English working class. One could now expect a resurgence of Chartism. But there the English bourgeoisie led a masterstroke. It split the English proletariat, granted the organized workers the right to vote, detached them from the masses of the rest of the proletariat, and thus prevented the resurgence of Chartism. It did not possess a comprehensive program beyond the general right vote. As soon as this demand was met in a way that satisfied the militant sections of the working class, the ground for it had disappeared. It was not until the end of the century, when the English were struggling to crawl behind the workers of the European mainland, that they started to found an independent workers' party again. But they have long failed to grasp the practical significance of socialism for the full development of the proletariat's power and have refused to accept a program for their party because it could only be a socialist one! They waited until the logic of the facts forced it upon them.

Everywhere today the conditions are already given for the necessary unification of workers' movement and socialism. They were missing in the first decades of the nineteenth century.

At that time the workers were so defeated by the first onslaught of capitalism that they could hardly resist it. It was rare enough that they defended themselves, albeit in a primitive way. They lacked all possibilities for deeper societal studies.

The bourgeois socialists therefore saw in the misery spread by capitalism only one side, the oppressive one, not the other, the inciting one and the one spurring on the revolutionary rise of the proletariat. They believed there was only one factor capable of enforcing the liberation of the proletariat: bourgeois goodwill. They judged the bourgeoisie from their own position, believing that they could find in it enough good fellow-men to be able to carry out socialist measures.

Their socialist propaganda was also initially well received by the bourgeois philanthropists. On average, the bourgeois are not inhuman. The misery touches them, and as far as they do not profit from it, they would like to help. Meanwhile, as the *suffering* proletarian is viewed favorably, the *fighting* one is viewed harshly. They feel that he shakes at the root of their existence. The *begging* proletariat enjoys their sympathies, the *demanding* one drives them to outrage and wild enmity. So, the socialists found it very unpleasant that the labor movement threatened to rob them of the factor on which they relied most: the sympathies of the "well-meaning bourgeoisie" for the dispossessed.

The lower their confidence in the proletariat, which at the time generally still formed a very low mass, and the more clearly they recognized the inadequacy of the naïve labor movement, the more they saw a disturbing element in the labor movement. Thus, they often came to turn against the workers' movement, proving, for example, how useless the unions were by simply trying to raise wages rather than fight the wage system itself, the root of all evil.

Gradually, however, a reversal was taking place. In the forties, the labor movement was ready to produce a series of highly gifted minds who seized socialism and recognized in it the proletarian science of society. These workers already knew from their own experience that they could not count on the philanthropy of the bourgeoisie. They recognized that the proletariat had to free itself. In addition, bourgeois socialists realized that the generosity of the bourgeoisie could not be relied upon. Admittedly, they did not gain confidence in the proletariat. The movement appeared to them only as a destructive force that threatened all culture. They believed that only bourgeois intelligentsia could build a socialist society, but saw the driving force behind it no longer in *compassion* for the tolerating but in *fear* of the storming proletariat. They already recognized its tremendous power and understood that the labor movement necessarily emerged from the capitalist mode of production, that it would grow more and more within that mode of production. They hoped that the fear of the growing labor movement would cause the intelligent bourgeoisie to take away its dangerousness through socialist measures.

This was a tremendous advance, but the union of socialism and the workers' movement could still not spring from this latter view. Despite the genius of some of them, the socialist workers lacked the comprehensive knowledge needed to establish a new, higher theory of socialism in which it was organically linked to the labor movement. They could only adopt the old bourgeois socialism, utopianism, and adapt it to their needs.

The proletarian socialists who were most far-reaching were those who followed Chartism or the French Revolution. In particular, the latter gained great importance in the history of socialism. The Great Revolution had clearly shown the importance that the conquest of state power can have for the liberation of a class. In this revolution, however, thanks to strange circumstances, a powerful political organization, the Jacobin Club, had also managed to dominate all of Paris and all of France through a reign of terror by the petty bourgeoisie, who were then strongly displaced by proletarian elements. Even during the revolution itself, Babeuf had already drawn the consequences of this in a purely proletarian sense and tried, by a conspiracy, to conquer state power for a communist organization and make it subservient.

The memory of this had never died in the French workers. The conquest of state power early became the means for the proletarian socialists to gain the strength to carry out socialism. But given the weakness and immaturity of the proletariat, they knew of no other way to conquer state power than the coup d'état of a number of conspirators to unleash the revolution. Blanqui is best known among the representatives of this thought in France. Weitling represented similar ideas in Germany.

Other socialists also took up the French Revolution. But the coup appeared to them to be a less than suitable means of overthrowing the rule of capital. Neither did the direction just mentioned count on the strength of the workers' movement. It helped itself by overlooking the extent to which the petty bourgeoisie was based on the same basis of private ownership of the means of production as capital, by believing that the proletarians could carry out their confrontation with the capitalists without being disturbed by the petty bourgeoisie, the "people," even with its assistance. One needed only the republic and universal suffrage to induce the power of the state to socialist measures.

This superstition of some republicans, whose most distinguished representative was Louis Blanc, found a counterpart in Germany in the monarchical superstition of social kingship, as cherished by a few professors and other ideologues, such as Rodbertus.

This monarchical state socialism was always only a quirk, here and there also a demagogic phrase. It has never gained serious practical significance. However, this was not the case with the directions represented by Blanqui and Louis Blanc. They gained the strength to rule Paris in the days of the February Revolution of 1848.

In the person of Proudhon they acquired a tremendous critic. He doubted the proletariat, the state, and the revolution. He recognized well that the proletariat must free itself, but he also saw that if it fought for its liberation, it must also take up the struggle with the state and for state power, for even the purely economic struggle depended on the state power, as the workers at the time felt at every turn the lack of any freedom to associate. Since Proudhon now regarded the struggle for state power as hopeless, he advised the proletariat to refrain from any struggle in its emancipatory efforts and to apply only the means of peaceful organization, such as exchange banks, insurance funds, and similar institutions. He had just as little sympathy for trade unions as he had for politics.

Thus, the workers' movement and socialism, and all attempts to bring the two into a closer relationship, formed a chaos of the most diverse currents in the decade in which Marx and Engels formed their point of view and method. Each current had discovered a piece of what was right, yet none was willing to form them into a totality, with each sooner or later having to end in failure.

What these directions were unable to do was achieved by the materialistic conception of history, which thus, in addition to its great significance for science, gained no less significance for the actual development of society. It facilitated the revolution of one and the other.

Like the socialists of their time, Marx and Engels also recognized that the workers' movement appears inadequate when it is contrasted with socialism and one asks: what is the more appropriate means with which to provide the proletariat with a secure existence and abolition of all exploitation? The workers' movement (trade unions, the struggle for the right to vote, etc.), or socialism? But they also realized that this question was completely wrong. Socialism, the secure existence of the proletariat, and the abolition of all exploitation are synonymous. The question is only this: how does the proletariat get to socialism? And there the doctrine of class struggle answered: through the labor movement.

It may not be able to provide the proletariat with a secure existence and the abolition of all exploitation, but it is the indispensable means not only to save the individual proletarians from sinking into misery, but also to give the whole class ever greater power — intellectual, economic, and political power, power that is always growing, even if at the same time the exploitation of the proletariat is increasing. The labor movement must be measured not according to its significance for restricting exploitation, but according to its significance for increasing the power of the proletariat. Not from Blanquist conspiracy, but also not from the state socialism of Louis Blanc or Rodbertus, nor from the peaceful organizations of Proudhon, but only from the class struggle, which has to last for decades, even generations, does the strength arise which can and must seize the state in the form of the democratic republic and finally bring about the breakthrough of socialism in it. To lead the economic and political class struggle, to cultivate its detailed work zealously, but also to fill it with the thoughts of a far-sighted socialism, to thereby unite the organizations and activities of the proletariat uniformly and harmoniously into a tremendous whole that swells more and more irresistibly — according to Marx and

Engels, this is the task of everyone who, whether he is a proletarian or not, takes the standpoint of the proletariat and wants to liberate it.

The growth of the power of the proletariat itself, however, is in the last analysis based on the displacement of the pre-capitalist, petty-bourgeois modes of production by the capitalist one, which increases the number of proletarians, concentrates them, increases their indispensability for the whole of society, but at the same time also creates in increasingly concentrated capital the preconditions for the social organization of production, which no longer is arbitrarily invented by the utopians but develops from capitalist reality.

Through this train of thought, Marx and Engels have created the foundation on which social democracy rises, the foundation on which the struggling proletariat of the entire world, from which it began its glorious triumphal march, is increasingly based.

This achievement was hardly possible as long as socialism did not have its own science, independent of bourgeois science. The socialists before Marx and Engels were mostly very familiar with the science of political economy, but they adopted it uncritically in the form in which it had been created by bourgeois thinkers, and differed from them only in that they drew other, proletarian conclusions from it.

It was only Marx who undertook a completely independent study of the capitalist mode of production, who showed how much deeper and clearer it can be when viewed from the proletarian point of view, rather than from the bourgeois point of view. For the proletarian standpoint stands outside and above it, not in it. Only he who regards capitalism as a temporary form makes it possible to fully grasp its particular historical peculiarity.

This feat was performed by Marx in his work *Capital* (1867), after he had already presented his new socialist point of view with Engels in *The Communist Manifesto* (1848).

Thus, the proletarian struggle for emancipation had received a scientific basis of a magnitude and strength which no revolutionary class before it had possessed. But of course, no one had yet been given such a gigantic task as the modern proletariat; it had to rethink the whole world that capitalism had thrown out of its seams. Fortunately, it is not Hamlet, it does not greet this task with woe. From its immense size it draws immense confidence and strength.

VI
Summary of Theory and Practice

We have now looked at the most important achievements Marx made in his association with Engels. But the picture of their work would remain incomplete if we did not point to another aspect which characterizes it to an outstanding degree: the link between theory and practice.

To bourgeois thought, of course, this seems to be another patch on the shining shield of its scientific greatness, before which even bourgeois scholarship must bend, albeit reluctantly, grumbling and without understanding. If they had been mere theorists, parlor scholars who were content to discuss their theories in a language incomprehensible to ordinary people and in inaccessible folios, this could have gone further. But the fact that their science was born out of struggle and again serves the struggle, the struggle against the existing order, has robbed them of their impartiality and clouded their honesty.

This miserable view can only imagine a fighter as a lawyer, whose knowledge should serve nothing but to give him arguments to refute the other party. It has no idea that no one has a greater need for truth than a true fighter in a terrible fight, in which he has only the prospect of surviving if he recognizes his situation, tools, and his prospects in full clarity. The judges who interpret the laws of the state can be deceived by the tricks of a sophist who dominates legal science. The necessary laws of nature, on the other hand, can only be recognized, not duped nor bribed.

A fighter who takes this point of view will only draw from the fierceness of the fight an increased urge for undisguised truth; but also the urge not to keep the truth for oneself, but to communicate it to one's comrades-in-arms.

Thus Engels also writes of the time period between 1845 and 1848, within which he and Marx had won their new scientific results, that they had no intention at all of whispering these results "in thick books exclusively to the 'learned' world." Rather, they immediately contacted proletarian organizations in order to propagate their point of view and the tactics corresponding to it. In this way they succeeded in winning over one of the most important of the then-revolutionary proletarian associations, the international "Communist League," for their principles, which were then expressed a few weeks before the February Revolution of 1848 in *The Communist Manifesto*, which was to become the "guide" of the proletarian movement of all countries.

The revolution called on Marx and Engels from Brussels, where they were staying, first in Paris, then in Germany, where they were for some time completely absorbed in revolutionary practice.

The decline of the revolution forced them from 1850 on, much against their will, to devote themselves entirely to theory. But when the workers' movement revived in the early 1860s, Marx — for Engels was initially hindered by private circumstances — was immediately again able to intervene with full force in the practical movement. He did this in the International Workingmen's Association, founded in 1864, which was soon to become a spectre for the whole of bourgeois Europe.

The laughable police mindset, with which even bourgeois democracy suspects every proletarian movement, made the International appear as a tremendous conspiracy society which had as its sole task the organization of riots and coups. In reality, it pursued its aims in full publicity: that of uniting all the proletarian forces into joint but also into independent action, detached from bourgeois politics and bourgeois thought, with the aim of expropriating capital, of the proletariat conquering all the political and economic means of power of the possessing classes. The most important and decisive step is the conquest of political power, but the economic emancipation of the working classes is the ultimate goal "to which every political movement must submit as a mere aid."

Marx considers organization to be the most noble tool of the proletarian development of power.

"The proletarians possess an element of success," he said in the inaugural address, "their numbers. But this only becomes significant if it is united by an organization and led toward a conscious goal."

Without a goal, no organization. The common goal alone can unite the different individuals into a common organization. On the other hand, the diversity of goals is as divisive as the unity of goals is unifying.

Precisely because of the importance of organization for the proletariat, everything depends on the kind of goal that is set for it. This goal is of the greatest practical importance. Nothing is more impractical than the apparently realist view that the movement is everything and the goal nothing. Is organization then also nothing and the unorganized movement everything?

Even before Marx, socialists had set goals for the proletariat. But these had only caused sectarianism, divided the proletarians, since each of these socialists put the main emphasis on the particular way of solving the social problem they had invented. So many solutions, so many sects.

Marx gave no particular solution. He resisted all the challenges of becoming "positive," of setting out in detail the measures by which the proletariat should be emancipated. In the International, he valued in organization only the general goal that every proletarian should make his own the economic liberation of his class; and the path he showed to that end was one that every proletarian already demonstrated in his class instinct: the economic and political class struggle.

Above all, it was the trade-union form of organization that Marx propagated in the

International; it appeared to be the form most likely to permanently unite large masses. He also saw the cadres of the workers' party existing in the trade unions.

No less eagerly did he pursue their imbuement with the spirit of class struggle — and their development to understand the conditions under which the expropriation of the capitalist class and the liberation of the proletariat was possible — than he pursued the expansion of trade-union organization itself.

He had to overcome great resistance, especially among the most advanced workers, who were still filled with the spirit of the old socialists and looked down on the unions with disdain because they did not challenge the wage system. They saw this as a departure from the right path, which they saw in the establishment of organizations in which the wage system was to be directly overcome, such as productive cooperatives. If, nevertheless, trade-union organization on the continent of Europe has made rapid progress since the second half of the 1860s, it owes it above all to the International and to the influence that Marx exerted on it and through it.

But the trade unions for Marx were not ends in themselves, but only a means to the end of class struggle against the capitalist order. He resisted those trade union leaders who tried to make the unions averse to this purpose — whether for limited personal or trade-union reasons — with the most vigorous resistance, as with the English trade-union officials who began to cheat with the liberals.

As indulgent and tolerant Marx was towards the proletarian *masses*, he was exceedingly strict towards those who acted as their *leaders*. This was primarily true of their theorists.

Into the proletarian organization, Marx warmly welcomed every proletarian who came with the honest intention of joining in the class struggle, no matter what views the entrant otherwise paid homage to, what theoretical motivations drove him, what arguments he used; no matter whether he was an atheist or a good Christian, whether Proudhonian, Blanquist, Weitlingian, or Lassallean, whether he understood the value of theory or considered it completely superfluous, etc.

Of course, he was not indifferent as to whether he was dealing with clear-thinking or confused workers. He considered it an important task to enlighten them, but he would have thought it wrong to repel workers and keep them away from the organization because their thought was confused. He placed full trust in the power of class antagonism and the logic of class struggle, which had to put every proletarian on the right path once he had joined an organization that served a real proletarian class struggle.

But he behaved differently toward people who came to the proletariat as teachers when they spread views that were likely to disrupt the power and unity of this class struggle. Against such elements he knew no tolerance. As a relentless critic, he confronted them, even if their intentions were the best; their work seemed to him in any case ruinous — that is, if it produced results at all and did not prove to be a mere waste of energy.

Thanks to this, Marx has always been one of the most hated men; most hated not only by the bourgeoisie, which feared in him its most dangerous enemy, but also by all the sectarians, inventors, educated councils of confusion, and similar elements in the socialist camp, who, the more painfully they felt his criticism, became the more outraged by his "intolerance," his "authoritarianism," his "papacy," his "heretical courts."

With the adoption of his views, we Marxists have also inherited this position, and we are proud of it. Only those who feel they are weak complain about the "intolerance" of a purely literary critique. Nobody is criticized more harshly, maliciously, than Marx and Marxism. But so far, no Marxist has thought of singing a sad song about the intolerance of our literary opponents. We are too sure of our cause for that.

What does not leave us indifferent, on the other hand, is the displeasure that the proletarian masses sometimes express about the literary feuds fought out between Marxism and its critics. This displeasure expresses a very justified need: the need for unity in the class struggle, for the combination of all proletarian elements into a great independent mass, the fear of divisions that could weaken the proletariat.

The workers know very well what strength they draw from their unity; it stands above theoretical clarity, and they curse theoretical discussions when they threaten to lead to divisions. Rightly so, for the pursuit of theoretical clarity would achieve the opposite of what it is supposed to achieve if it weakened rather than strengthened the proletarian class struggle.

A Marxist who would continue a theoretical disagreement to the point of splitting a proletarian fighting organization would not, however, be acting as a Marxist, in the sense of the Marxist doctrine of class struggle, for which every step of real movement is more important than a dozen programs.

Marx and Engels have already set out their view of the Marxist position within proletarian organizations in *The Communist Manifesto* in the section entitled "Proletarians and Communists." The communists were then about the same as what are now called Marxists.

It says:

"What is the relationship between the communists and the proletariat?

The communists do not form a separate party to the other workers' parties.

They have no interests separate from the interests of the entire proletariat.

They do not establish special principles according to which they want to model the proletarian movement.

The communists differ from the other proletarian parties only in that, on the one hand, they emphasize and assert the common interests of the entire proletariat, which are independent of nationality, in the various national struggles of the proletarians [i.e. limited to the individual states] and, on the other hand, they always represent the interests of the entire movement during the various stages of development through which the struggle between the proletariat and the bourgeoisie passes.

The communists are thus practically the most decisive, ever-expanding part of the workers' parties of all countries; theoretically, they have the insight into the conditions, the course, and the general results of the proletarian movement ahead of the rest of the mass of the proletariat.

The next purpose of the communists is the same as that of all other proletarian parties: formation of the proletariat into a class, overthrow of bourgeois rule, conquest of political power by the proletariat.

The theoretical propositions of the communists are by no means based on ideas, on principles invented or discovered by this or that do-gooder. They are only general expressions of the actual conditions of an existing class struggle, of a historical movement going on under our eyes."

In the time since this was written, many things have changed so that these sentences can no longer be applied to every letter. In 1848 there were still no large, unified workers' parties with comprehensive socialist programs, and alongside Marxist theory there were many other, much more widespread socialist theories.

Today, among the struggling proletariat united in mass parties, only one socialist theory is still alive: the Marxist theory. Not all members of the workers' parties are Marxists; even less are all educated Marxists. But those among them who do not recognize Marxist theory have no theory at all. Either they deny the necessity of every theory and every program, or they brew a universal socialism together with a few Marxist chunks from pieces of the pre-Marxist ways of thinking that we have just come to know and that have not yet completely disappeared, which has the advantage that you can omit from it everything that doesn't fit into your agenda at the moment, and take everything into it that seems usable at the moment, which is far more convenient than consistent Marxism, but fails completely where theory becomes most important. It is enough for the usual purposes of popular agitation, but it fails when it comes to finding one's way in reality in the face of new, unexpected phenomena. Precisely because of its flexibility and softness, one cannot make a building out of it that defies all storms. But it also cannot form a roadmap which guides the seeker, since it is entirely determined by the personal momentary needs of his bearers.

Today Marxism must no longer assert itself in the proletariat against other socialist views. Its critics no longer oppose it with other theories, but only with doubts about the necessity of either theory at all or a consistent theory. There are only words, phrases like those of "dogmatism," "orthodoxy," and the like, not closed new systems, which are held against it in the proletarian movement.

For us Marxists today, however, this is just one more reason to report on any attempt to form a special Marxist sect within the workers' movement that is detached from the other strata of the fighting proletariat. Like Marx, we see it as our task to unite the *entire* proletariat into one fighting organism. Within this organism, however, it will always be our goal to remain "the most practical, decisive, and ever-advancing part" that "has the insight into the conditions, the course, and the general results of the proletarian movement ahead of the rest of the mass of the proletariat" — that is, we will always strive to achieve the highest level of practical energy and theoretical knowledge that can be achieved with the given means. Only in this, in the superiority of our achievements, which the superiority of the Marxist standpoint enables us to achieve, do we want to occupy a special position in the overall organism of the proletariat organized as a class party, which, incidentally, wherever unconscious Marxism already fulfills it, is more and more pushed into its tracks by the logic of the facts.

But hardly a Marxist or Marxist group has ever caused a split because of purely theoretical differences. Where divisions occurred, they were always caused by *practical*, tactical, or organizational differences, not *theoretical* differences, and theory simply became the scapegoat onto whom all committed sins were laid.

For instance, the struggle by a part of the French socialists against an alleged Marxist intolerance is, when viewed in the light of day, only a struggle by a couple of literary critics and parliamentarians who are outraged by proletarian discipline. They demand discipline only for the great masses, but not for such enlightened beings as themselves. The defenders of proletarian discipline have always been the Marxists, and they have shown themselves to be dutiful students of their master.

Marx has not only theoretically shown the way in which the proletariat is most likely to achieve its high goal, he also made practical progress along this path. Through his work in the International he has become exemplary for all our practical activity.

Not only as a thinker, but also as a role model should we celebrate Marx, or rather, what is more, in his sense, study him. We draw no less wealth from the history of his personal effectiveness than from his theoretical discussions.

And he became exemplary in his work not only through his knowledge, his superior intellect, but also through his boldness, his tirelessness, which was paired with the greatest kindness and selflessness, and the most unshakable equanimity.

Whoever wants to learn of his boldness, read of his trial in Cologne on February 9, 1849, in which he was charged for his call to armed resistance and in which he explained the necessity of a new revolution. His goodness and selflessness is testified to by the active concern which he, even when living in the greatest misery, showed for his comrades, whom he always thought of rather than himself, after the collapse of the revolution of 1848, and after the fall of the Paris Commune of 1871. His whole life was finally an unbroken chain of tests which only a man whose tirelessness and unshakeability far exceeding the usual measure could have stood up to.

Beginning with his work in the *Rheinische Zeitung* (1842), he was rushed from country to country until the revolution of 1848 promised him the beginning of a victorious revolution. By its fall, he saw himself thrown back into political and personal misery, which seemed all the more hopeless, since in exile, on the one hand, bourgeois democracy boycotted him, and on the other hand, a part of the communists themselves fought him because he was not revolutionary enough for them, despite the fact that many of his faithful comrades were buried in Prussian fortresses for many years.

Then finally came a glimmer of hope, the International, but after a few years it vanished again by the fall of the Paris Commune, soon followed by the dissolution of the International and inner turmoil. It had fulfilled its task brilliantly, but it was precisely because of this that the proletarian movements of the individual countries had become more independent. The more it grew, the more the International needed a more elastic form of organization that would give the individual national organizations more leeway. At the same time, however, when this became most necessary, the English trade union leaders who wanted to join the liberals felt constrained by the tendencies of class struggle, while in the romantic countries Bakuninist anarchism rebelled against the participation of the workers in politics, phenomena which urged the General Council of the International to exercise its centralist powers most sharply at the time when the federalism of the organization became more necessary than ever. It was this contradiction that failed the proud ship whose steering wheel Karl Marx had in his hands.

This became a bitter disappointment for Marx. Of course, then came the brilliant rise of German social democracy and the strengthening of the revolutionary movement in Russia. In turn, the Anti-Socialist Law put an end to this brilliant rise, and Russian terrorism also reached its peak in 1881. From then on it went rapidly downhill.

Thus, Marx's political activity was an unbroken chain of failures and disappointments, and no less his scientific activity. His life's work, *Capital*, for which he had great expectations, apparently remained unnoticed and ineffective. Even in his own party, it was little understood until the early eighties.

Marx died on the threshold of that time when the fruits of what he had sowed during the most furious storms and sunless, gloomy times would finally ripen. He died when the time came that the proletarian movement seized the whole of Europe and everywhere filled it with its spirit, placed itself on its foundations, and thus began a period of victorious growth of the proletariat; and this growth does so brilliantly stand out from the time when Marx fought for his ideas in the class as a lonely, little-understood, but much-hated fighter against a world of enemies.

As discouraging, indeed downright bleak, this situation would have become for any ordinary man, Marx never let it rob him of his cheerful equanimity, never of his proud confidence. He so surpassed his fellow men, so far overlooked them, that he saw clearly the land of promise which the great mass of his fellow men was not able to foresee. It was his scientific greatness, the depth of his theory from which he drew the best strength of his character, in which his steadfastness and his confidence were rooted, which kept him free from all fluctuations and attitudes, from that unsteady feeling of exuberance which rejoices sky-high today and tomorrow is saddened to death.

From this source we must also draw. Then we can be sure that, in the great and difficult struggles of our days, we will stand at the ready and develop the utmost strength of which we are capable. Then we may expect to reach our goal sooner than would otherwise be possible. The banner of the liberation of the proletariat, and thus of all mankind — which Marx has unfolded, which he carried forward for more than a lifetime, in a constant onslaught, never tiring, never despairing — will be victoriously planted on the ruins of the capitalist stronghold by the fighters he has taught.